IT'S TIME TO LEARN ABOUT CORALS

It's Time to Learn about Corals

Walter the Educator

Silent King Books
A WhichHead Entertainment Imprint

Copyright © 2025 by Walter the Educator

All rights reserved. No part of this book may be reproduced in any manner whatsoever without written per- mission except in the case of brief quotations embodied in critical articles and reviews.

First Printing, 2024

Disclaimer

This book is a literary work; the story is not about specific persons, locations, situations, and/or circumstances unless mentioned in a historical context. Any resemblance to real persons, locations, situations, and/or circumstances is coincidental. This book is for entertainment and informational purposes only. The author and publisher offer this information without warranties expressed or implied. No matter the grounds, neither the author nor the publisher will be accountable for any losses, injuries, or other damages caused by the reader's use of this book. The use of this book acknowledges an understanding and acceptance of this disclaimer.

It's Time to Learn about Corals is a collectible early learning book by Walter the Educator suitable for all ages belonging to Walter the Educator's Time to Eat Book Series. Collect more books at WaltertheEducator.com

USE THE EXTRA SPACE TO TAKE NOTES AND DOCUMENT YOUR MEMORIES

CORALS

Down in the ocean, so deep and so blue,

It's Time to Learn about

Corals

Lives a bright coral reef with a colorful view.

It's home to sea creatures both tiny and grand,

In a wiggly, wavy, underwater land.

Coral looks like a rock, but it's really alive,

It builds big reefs where sea critters thrive.

They come in bright colors—red, orange, and green,

The prettiest homes you have ever seen!

Here comes a clownfish, orange, white, and small,

It hides in sea anemones, safe from all.

They tickle and sting with their wavy arms,

But to clownfish, they bring no harm.

A parrotfish munches on coral with cheer,

Its beak-like mouth chomps loud and clear.

It poops out sand, which makes the beach grow

A funny fish fact you might not know!

It's Time to Learn about

Corals

An octopus hides in a coral-side cave,

With eight twisty arms that swirl and wave.

It can squirt ink when it's time to flee,

And change its color to blend with the sea!

Sea turtles glide with flippers so wide,

Like gentle giants they softly slide.

They snack on sea grass and jellyfish too,

And lay eggs on beaches under skies so blue.

Tiny shrimp clean up with their little claws,

They nibble dead skin from a fish's jaws.

Cleaner shrimp help keep the reef neat,

Their dancing feelers make them sweet!

Starfish creep slowly on five strong feet,

They cling to the reef where it's rocky and neat.

If one arm is lost, it can grow a new

It's Time to Learn about

Corals

A star-shaped friend with a magic trick too!

Jellyfish float with a soft, glowing gleam,

They drift with the current, like a lazy dream.

Their tentacles sting, so you must beware,

But they look like lanterns lighting the air.

So many creatures, from big to small,

Live in the coral and love it all.

Protect the reef, keep the oceans clean,

It's Time to Learn about

Corals

So the coral sea stays bright and green!

ABOUT THE CREATOR

Walter the Educator is one of the pseudonyms for Walter Anderson. Formally educated in Chemistry, Business, and Education, he is an educator, an author, a diverse entrepreneur, and he is the son of a disabled war veteran. "Walter the Educator" shares his time between educating and creating. He holds interests and owns several creative projects that entertain, enlighten, enhance, and educate, hoping to inspire and motivate you. Follow, find new works, and stay up to date with Walter the Educator™

at WaltertheEducator.com

www.ingramcontent.com/pod-product-compliance
Lightning Source LLC
LaVergne TN
LVHW010412070526
838199LV00064B/5267